VISIONS OF LIFE

Emma-Jane Welsh

MINERVA PRESS

LONDON

ATLANTA MONTREUX SYDNEY

VISIONS OF LIFE
Copyright © Emma-Jane Welsh 1998

ISBN 0 75410 143 6

First Published 1998 by
MINERVA PRESS
195 Knightsbridge
London SW7 1RE

Printed in Great Britain for Minerva Press

VISIONS OF LIFE

About the Author

Emma-Jane Welsh was born in Bathgate, West Lothian, Scotland, in 1982. She is currently attending Saint Kentigerns Academy in Blackburn, as she is still a student. Before this, she went to St Mary's Primary School in Bathgate.

Her hobbies include playing the violin and piano, Highland dancing and, of course, writing poetry!

Emma has had several poems published in anthologies and a limerick published. This is the first book of her own.

People who have encouraged her include: Annette Welsh (mum), Margaret Casey (gran), Patricia and John Ross (aunt and uncle), Mr C. Giles (teacher), Imogen Stone, Caroline Dunne, Stacey Boyle, Vicci Sinclair, Jenna Gunn, Denise Forrest, Gillian Ferry, Morna Kelly and Sarah Monoghan (friends), Mr and Mrs Johnstone, and Marianne Smith (sister). (There are many more people but we can't mention them all.)

Emma-Jane's philosophical statement is: To dream of things that cannot be is to live them for a little while.

Contents

This is The Life I Wanted to Live

I left because I wanted to leave.
I know it's hard for you to believe
But this is the life I wanted to live.

I know you think I've been led astray
But this is where I want to stay.
The rough life attracts me,
Nothing distracts me.
I have to be tough to live on the street,
Sometimes I get quite badly beat
But this is the life I wanted to live.

I move about from time to time
If I feel there's too much crime.
I go wherever the wind blows –
It's the best thing for it, I suppose.
I drift along like a paper bag
I know I shouldn't really brag
But this is the life I wanted to live.

Alone

If you're alone with nowhere to go,
You think you are hopeless, 'cause people say so.
Everyone keeps picking on you
And you keep wondering what you will do.
Everything goes wrong, nothing goes right
And it could destroy you if you don't hold on tight.
No one will listen, no one will care;
The stress is just getting too hard to bear.
They say life goes on but it's not always true,
When someone's as unhappy, as unhappy as you.

Don't Change

There is no point in trying to be someone you are not,
You don't have to change, so get rid of that thought.
You don't have to be a 'number one' star,
Just be happy with who you are.
Don't worry about what other people say
You're the one who matters, they'll soon go away.

The Storm

As lightning strikes and thunder roars,
And the stormy rain harshly pours,
The strong wind blows making a whistling sound
And the leaves on the trees fall to the ground;
In the woods I walk around
Never to be seen, never to be found.
I was so sure I heard someone shout
But now my mind is full of doubt.
It's very quiet now the storm's died down
In this cold and lonesome town,
Now I'll walk right out of sight
Into the silence of the night.

Homeless People

Homeless people on the street
Begging from people that they meet,
They could freeze or starve out there,
Though no one ever seems to care
When winter comes they won't survive
But who will notice if they're not alive?
They have no family, nowhere to stay,
People look, then look away.
Sometimes people stop and stare
Then walk away, they don't care
When they have nothing left, they have to steal,
But the police don't care how they feel –
They just lock them up and then walk away.
Jail's the only place they're welcome to stay.

Walking Along the River Bank

The water is stirring quietly as the fish swim about,
The baby birds in their nests slowly fly out,
It was so quiet before, but now the world has awoke
As the birds start to chirp, and the frogs start to croak.
There's a harp being played but there's no one else here,
I thought I understood but now nothing seems clear;
I'm away from the world, in a world of my own
But where I am will never be known

Under the Sea

There's a magical world
Under the sea.
There is a locked door –
Only we have the key.
Inside that door
Is a wonderful place,
Where dolphins fly
And jellyfish race.
There are lots of mermaids
Swimming about
And also lobsters,
Crabs and trout.
You'll find some starfish
Here and there
And there's always
Seaweed everywhere.
There are magical leaves
That take you far, far away –
You can go where you want
They do what you say.
Everyone loves it under the sea,
It's full of magic and mystery.

It Was Only a Dream

I thought I was dying
I was sure it was true,
I couldn't breath
There was nothing I could do.
Nothing made sense
Nothing seemed right
All I could do was keep holding on tight.
My hands were aching
My head was pounding
I couldn't hold on anymore.
I was so high up
It was such a height
But suddenly I awoke with a fright.
Just when I was about to let out a scream
I suddenly realised it was only a dream.

The Perfect Coin

The perfect coin shines in the light,
The bronze glow is a perfect sight,
It's perfectly smooth and perfectly round
When it falls, it makes a jingling sound.
You'd think it would be valuable, but really it's not
You can't buy much with it, it's not worth a lot.
It's just so perfect, it's as perfect as can be
It's just such a pity that it's only 1p.

The Sorcerer

The genius of sorcery,
Master of spells,
Creates such magic
Which no one foretells.
You may think that these spells
Must be a trick,
But the wonders he produces
Are pure magic.

Inside the sorcerer
The magic unwinds,
Magic so powerful,
Magic of all kinds.
The magic explodes
With an earth-shuddering boom
It turns chairs into tables
As it races around the room.

Books jump on to the table
And dance about with glee,
At last they are able to move –
The magic has set them free.
Pieces of paper fly about
Like a flock of frantic birds;
Then suddenly everything stops
As they hear the magic words.

The tables turn back into chairs,
The books jump into their case
The pieces of paper float down
And go back to their own place.
Now the room is quiet
It's as tranquil as the sky,
For the sorcerer is the ruler
And no one would dare defy.

Waiting

She waited for someone to speak
Before she opened her mouth.
She waited for others to phone
Before she would phone herself.
She waited until it was sunny
Before she went outside.
She waited her whole life
For a life that didn't happen.

The Poor Old Drunken Man

The poor old drunken man
Staggers down the hill.
No one cares about him,
No one ever will.

It's hard for people to realise
The problems this man has had,
Before his addiction started,
He wasn't all that bad.

He lost his wife and family
In a fire sometime last year.
Now he cannot cope,
So he drowns himself with beer.

He is alone in the world.
He doesn't have friends.
But can you really blame them,
With the message that he sends?

The expression on his face
Says he's as happy as can be.
But the message in his eyes
Tells a different story.

The money that he has
All gets spent on drink.
He drinks himself to sleep
So he will not have to think.

He won't have to bother
About the sorrows in his mind.
He won't have to worry
About problems of that kind.

But this time he has drunk too much
He will not feel anymore pain;
At last his life has ended
He will never wake again.

*(Dedicated to my English teacher,
Mr C. Giles, for all his help.)*

He's Not What You Think

He is like an angel in your eyes.
Why can't you see beyond his disguise?
When will you realise that you have been deceived?
With all the lies that he has told, the lies that you believed.
Trying to warn you is a difficult task,
You refuse to see beyond his mask.
As he sinks deeper into his pretence,
You continue to come to his defence.
I don't want to be in the middle of this mess.
I don't want to be here, to see your distress.
Because you will find out soon about all his deeds.
You will find out soon about the double life that he leads.

Cheer Up!

Cheer up! The world is on your side.
Don't conceal that smile you love to hide.
Stop pretending that your life is so bad.
Think of the lives that others have had.
If you look around, you will see people dying.
If you look around, you will see people crying.
Now look at yourself, what do you see?
Are you as happy as you should be?
Hold on to your hopes, don't let them drift away.
Keep smiling, life gets better every day.
Pick up your dreams before they fall and shatter,
And don't worry about things that don't really matter.

Trapped Forever

'Stop! Stop! It's a big mistake!
Please listen! I'm still awake!
Can't you hear my muffled shout?
Please put me down and let me out.'

I can't explain this feeling of fear
When I scream and scream yet you cannot hear.
I need fresh air, that's what I crave
But I'm going down into my grave!

I hear you sprinkle the soil on top
And I scream and scream for you to stop.
'Please don't leave me to face my fate
If I don't get out I'll suffocate!'

But it's too late now, I can't survive
Because no one knows I'm still alive.
I must die slowly without a sound
For I'm trapped forever, underground.

A Husband's Devotion

Betty, I thank you for the part you have played;
By my side you have always stayed.
People like you are so hard to find
You have always been caring, you have always been kind.
For you are the one I know I can trust,
Whose halo contains not a speck of dust,
And you are an angel, you came from above.
I thank God in heaven for your unending love.

(Dedicated to Mr and Mrs Johnstone from Blackburn.)

Listen!

'Listen, Emma, listen!
Elements are arranged in...'
I walk up the hill and see a beautiful dragon.
Behind the dragon there is...
'Pay attention, Emma!
The valency of hydrogen is 1 because of the...'
I climb on to the dragon's back, and fly over the hills and...
'Emma, are you listening?'
'Yes, sir.'
'What did I just say?'
'Er, something about hydrogen?'
'No, I was talking about structural formulae.
Wake up, Emma, listen!'

The Spider

As I watch a spider crawl,
I see it crawling up the wall.
It's determined not to stop
Until it gets to the top.
It looks to me so very small
Yet it doesn't slip, nor does it fall.
So much effort must be tiring.
Determination is inspiring.
Now a web is being spun;
It takes some time until it's done,
But I know that when the web's complete
Every strand will indeed be neat.

I Wish I Had a Magic Carpet

I wish I had a magic carpet,
I could fly up in the sky –
I could flutter up and down
Just like a butterfly.

I wish I had a magic carpet,
It would save me so much time –
I could fly up to the mountain tops
And I wouldn't have to climb.

I wish I had a magic carpet
I could fly to work each day,
I could sail right through the traffic jams
And be there without delay.

I don't have a magic carpet.
I must drive to work each day.
I won't have a magic carpet –
But the thought won't go away.

I Need to Go On Holiday

I want to get away today,
I need to go on holiday.
I don't care if it's boat or plane,
I don't care if it's France or Spain,
But I need to go on holiday!

I want to be out in the sun,
Lying around, getting nothing done.
I just want to feel that I am free
To be on the beach, by the sea.
I just want to go on holiday!

I want to feel the soft, golden sand
Running through my open hand.
I think about this every year.
How I want to get away from here.
I just need to go on holiday!